Your Wildlife Pond

D1343958

by **Peter Sibley**

Illustrations by
Tessa Lovatt-Smith and **Lindis Colam-Johnson**

Contents

SGC

BOOKS

1. Why construct a pond?

There are many reasons for constructing a pond - one is that over the last 100 years over half of Britain's ponds have been drained, filled in or ruined by pollution. London has lost 99% of its ponds in this period. The result has been a tremendous loss of wildlife habitat; plants and animals once common are now rare. The only way to replace these lost ponds is by creating new ones. But ponds also have aesthetic and amenity value. People are attracted to rivers, lakes and ponds; a pond is a focal point in a garden. Many school grounds are rather featureless; a pond will add visual interest, colour and variety. Most villages had their Pond along with the Green, the Church and the Pub - putting in a wildlife pond has to be a marvellous way to get the village community together.

Part of the appeal of ponds lies in the question, what lives in there? A crystal clear pond holds no mystery. A pond is a small, self-contained world, totally different from the world we inhabit, and because of this, exotic and strange, especially to children. A pond constantly changes in response to the seasons, weather, the growth of plants and the activity of animals. In this, it demonstrates the cyclic rhythms of the natural world both daily and seasonally and also the longer sequence of ecological succession.

All of these aspects of a pond can be used to help children understand more about the world they live in, developing their power of observation and reasoning and acting as a source of inspiration for creative activities.

Lastly, the creation of a pond involves measuring, mapping, calculating, planning, research, costing, discussion of alternatives, usually some fund-raising, planting and a lot of co-operative hard, physical work! It is the kind of practical project, which can involve all sorts of people. School ponds, for example, succeed best when created jointly by pupils, parents and teachers, so that a collective sense of ownership results. A successful pond is something that creates a real sense of achievement, a group effort with positive, lasting results and which all members of the family, school or community group can contribute towards.

Having said all this, be warned, there are pitfalls! The purpose of this book is to help you avoid them and create an attractive, safe pond, full of life and interest. Most of what follows applies to any type of pond, including the ornamental garden pond with its fountain and gleaming goldfish, but from a conservation viewpoint, wildlife ponds are what is really needed. These allow many plant and animal species threatened by the bulldozer and the crop sprayer to find new habitats - in your own bit of land to be shared again with nature.

<table>
<tr><td>2.</td><td><h1>Planning your pond</h1></td></tr>
</table>

You have decided to go ahead and create a pond? Good for you, but before you start digging there are a few things to do.

1. Consultation

It is important to consult everyone who might be involved. For a garden pond, talk the whole idea over with the family, and perhaps even the neighbours. In a school pond project check with the LEA and the owners of the grounds: the governors, the head teacher, other teachers and perhaps most important, the caretaker. It is also a good idea to consult the parents and any groups who use the school (in the evening for instance). Asking people usually forestalls trouble and often brings offers of help. On areas of publicly owned ground, consult the appropriate council officers and departments. You may discover an existing but derelict pond site in your neighbourhood, and change your project from a new pond to a renovation! (Incidentally, ponds don't normally require planning permission, but neighbours can object to the environmental health department if they cause a nuisance.)

Plan One

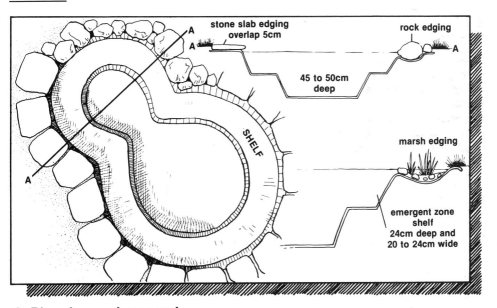

2. Planning and research

Before you start, pick your site (see the next chapter for help in this); decide on the shape, depth and profile of your pond (see next chapter again); and do a little careful test digging to find out what the ground is like.

Next, try to find out if your chosen area has any pipes, cables, sewers, drains, cesspits or old building foundations under it. (You never know what you will find; maps and plans are often inaccurate, but it is best to avoid unpleasant surprises - like power cables - if at all possible.) The services companies are normally helpful in checking their plans of underground pipes etc.

After that, try to calculate how much earth will need to be removed and approximately how long it may take; also decide what you'll do with it. Bear in mind that dug-out soil takes up more space than it previously occupied, because it is less compacted. A good idea is to build a mound or bank behind your pond; decide **where** first, to avoid shifting earth twice. If your calculations show that your mound is liable to over-top Ben Nevis, it may be advisable to make more modest plans (alternatively call your pond a reservoir and launch your own water company).

Other factors to consider are access to the pond, an easily observed site (for safety and to avoid misuse) and shelter.

Plan Two — rectangular using paving slabs

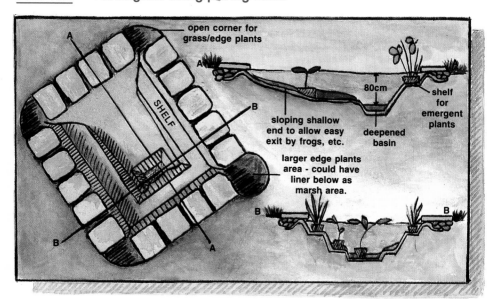

3. Costing

This is when you must try to get a rough idea of costs. Do not go to a landscaping company or professional gardening firm unless you feel very rich. (A communally built pond is usually better looked after anyway.) Instead, cost your raw materials, cement, sand, flagstones, bricks, plastic or butyl pond liner, glassfibre pond, puddling clay or whatever you decide to use and the tools you'll need. Cost the alternatives too, which will either confirm or change your plans. A good method of costing is to calculate rough quantities and then phone all the suppliers in the area, plus those who supply by post or carrier. (Make sure that you only ask for a quotation - do not use the term order or a lorry load of aggregate may get dumped on your drive!) You will probably find that prices vary considerably. Ask about discounts, particularly for community or school ponds. If the suppliers accept credit cards, they have to pay commission, so they'll probably give you a small discount for cash.

whirligig beetle

|⊢——⊣|
7mm

4. Type of pond

Ponds can be constructed in several ways and of many different materials; each has its advantages. You must decide which is most suitable.

Ponds can be constructed virtually anywhere - it is possible to build them above ground, even on flat roofs. A raised pond is a particularly good idea if you are concerned about wheelchair access, the safety of very small children or the elderly or infirm. It can also be a way to build a pond on a hard surface - rock, concrete, asphalt, tile or similar.

Plan Three

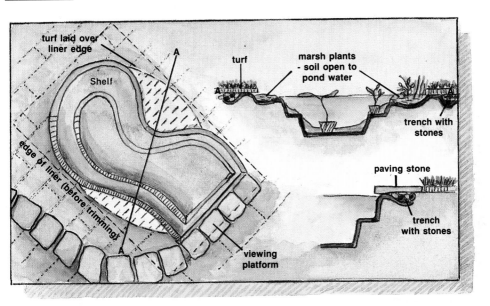

Another way to construct a pond is by damming a stream. If you do this, take professional advice and install a proper spillway to cope with rainstorms. This kind of pond will affect the local drainage and might create an extensive marshy area, excellent for wildlife but a problem if it affects neighbouring property.

Most ponds are, however, dug ponds lined with one of several materials. An *unlined* dug pond is not usually a good idea because the water level will fluctuate according to local weather conditions; it cannot be topped up artificially in dry conditions because the water will seep away until its level reaches that of the local water table.

Assuming then, that your pond is going to be a lined pond either above or below ground level, what are your options?

water scorpion

20mm

To take them in alphabetical order:-

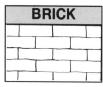

Brick

Brick is not a very practical material for constructing ponds because it is porous. It can make an excellent hard edge for a pond and weathers well. It is a good choice for the walls of a raised pond but it is better to use some other material to retain the water. Other problems are difficulties in building *natural* curves and slopes. Wet brick tends to become slimy, which can be dangerous. Waterproofing brick is difficult, and some compounds sold for this purpose are toxic. Mortar can also be toxic when fresh. So, brick is best avoided except as the outside wall of a lined, raised pond.

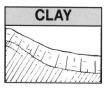

Clay

Clay is the traditional material for constructing ponds. It was used by the 18th and 19th century navigators or *navvies* to line the canals they built and it still retains the water to the present day. Most of the old ponds in Britain were man-made using clay, whether in fields, gardens or village greens.

It is the most natural lining material available, provides an excellent substrate for waterplants, is entirely non-toxic and helps to buffer acidic or alkaline water. Those comprise the benefits.

As for the drawbacks: in order to make clay linings impermeable they must be *puddled*. This means rammed, trampled or trodden down until the lumps of clay coalesce to form a seamless layer. This takes a lot of hard work and can only be done when the clay is wet, which makes it very messy.

The old time canal builders used to flatten the wet clay by thumping it with the backs of shovels and then driving herds of sheep and cattle along the bottom of the canal to tread it down. You could try holding a kid's welly boot disco in your new pond to get the same effect, but do remember how slippery wet clay is.

To get the best result, try to shape the clay to blocks that fit together closely and then wet them before *puddling*. It should be pretty obvious that you need a lot of hard working volunteers for this process. You also need a very large supply of suitable clay - which is extremely heavy. If a road is being constructed in the vicinity through a clay soil the contractor may be willing to deliver a lorry load free. Otherwise the cost of transport will be high. Bear in mind that the clay must be 5 to 10cm thick to be really waterproof. If your pond dries out and the clay cracks badly, you will have to repeat the puddling process.

If you do use clay, make sure that all slopes are shallow; climbing a wet clay bank is very difficult and could be fatal for a young child, an elderly, injured or drunken person. If you still decide to use puddled clay, I advise you to contact BTCV (see **Appendix**) for specialist help as they appear to be the only national organisation with recent experience of using this method.

Concrete

Concrete is a common material for constructing ponds. It is very versatile as it can be formed to almost any shape, can be textured, and is also entirely non-porous. It does however have a few drawbacks. It must be about 8 to 10cm thick for structural strength and for best results the whole pond should be poured in one operation. Shaping curves and

gnat pupa

|—|
5mm

slopes is not easy and *raw* or new concrete contains toxic substances that must be rinsed out by changing the water in the pond once or twice. (This can be solved by painting the surface a couple of times with a sealant such as *Silglaze.*) Vertical pond walls may be cracked by ice expansion in particularly hard winters and newly poured concrete can crumble if it freezes before it is properly set.

Having said this, many very successful ponds have been constructed of concrete and it has the advantage that it takes an extremely determined vandal to break it. The most usual source of any problem stems from not ensuring that the underlying soil is fully compacted; if it is not, the weight of the filled pond causes the concrete to settle unevenly and as a result, it cracks. Cracked ponds can be repaired but seldom completely successfully. Perhaps the best thing to do with a cracked concrete pond is to fill it with soil and create a bog garden, stocked with marsh plants.

GLASS FIBRE Glass fibre or GRP ponds

These are the commonest types of *ready-made* ponds - pre-formed structures that merely need a hole dug, or a raised structure built to fit them. In spite of their thin walls and light weight they are strong and long lasting, but have many drawbacks. They are limited in size and although they come in many shapes, never seem to be quite what you had in mind! They look artificial and are often pastel blue or other unnatural colour. The profile tends to be too steep and the interior surface is dangerously slippery. If the hole dug is not exactly the right shape they can warp and crack when filled and they are not damage proof. Glass fibre can however be repaired quite easily. Depth is limited and they provide poor *footholds* for plants. Overall they are of limited use for conservation purposes - but any pond is better than none and they do have the virtue of being quickly established. Frogs and toads don't seem to mind the artificiality and often breed in these ponds, though the steep sides can be a problem for them.

PLASTIC/BUTYL Plastic and butyl rubber liners

This is currently the most popular method of pond construction because of its ease, cost and flexibility. A variety of different pond liners are on the market, of different strengths, lifespans and costs. Basically though, you get what you pay for. A cheap plastic liner will not last very long (perhaps a few years). Thicker double-sided plastic liners are more expensive but will give 10 years (or more) service. The strongest, thickest butyl liners have an almost indefinite life. They can be made to fit almost any hole whatever the shape, are large enough to fill nearly any pond you can dig, and can be repaired if punctured.

Four main types of flexible liner are available from garden centres and suppliers (see **Appendix**):

Single sheet of PVC - the cheapest type available in several colours (stone, black, blue. etc.). The thicker the better, but like all PVC it is eventually weakened by sunlight (ultraviolet light). Plan your pond so that none of the PVC liner is exposed directly to light - cover edges with soil and paving stones. Black sheets are most resistant to u/v light. PVC sheets stretch to fit into corners of your pond, making installation quite simple and safe.

Double sheet of PVC - has the same eventual problems as single sheets, but the double layer sheet (often with different colours on the two sides) may be more durable.

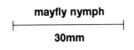

mayfly nymph

| 30mm |

Triple sheet of polyethylene (LDPE) - newest and best plastic liner: black, supple and more resistant to UV light, this heavy-duty material is usually somewhat cheaper than butyl.

Butyl rubber sheet - most expensive but also the best sort of liner. The black butyl (normal pond grade thickness is 0.75mm) is thicker and heavier than PVC and although not quite so stretchy, it conforms well to pool contours. Butyl is not affected by sunlight or bacterial growth and so need not be completely hidden. In practice, it is hard not to have a small amount of liner showing, but covering as far as possible with soil and paving stones etc. does give a more natural appearance.

The butyl liner should carry a 10+ year guarantee and will probably last twice as long. However, take care with *weeds*. Tough grasses and other weeds can and do burrow under pond edges and then push up **through** the liner. They will flourish in the mud while your pond leaks slowly away... The same problem will happen if you allow *couch grass* etc. to get established on the margins of your pond - it can push roots down through the liner. The answer is to keep pulling up unwanted weeds at the edge!

Working out the liner size - first decide how deep your pool will be. Small ponds should be around 40 to 50cm deep (in their deepest part - the pond floor should not normally be simply *flat*) and larger ponds up to 80cm deep. Only lakes need to be any deeper, so resist the temptation to make that huge hole!

Now work out the dimensions of your liner:

Length is the overall length of the pond plus *twice* the maximum depth.
Width is the overall width of the pond plus *twice* the maximum depth.

This formula will give sufficient surplus liner for the overlap at the pond edge, because of the sloping pool walls.

The biggest drawback of a pond liner is that it is not vandal proof. Precautions can be taken to protect pond liners and care must be exercised in the construction of the pond to ensure a long life. Although not perfect, pond liners are probably the best option for most ponds, though in some circumstances concrete or other materials may have advantages.

Constructing an overflow and soakaway

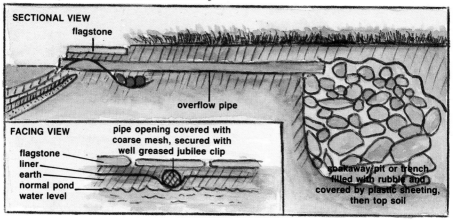

SECTIONAL VIEW
flagstone
overflow pipe

FACING VIEW
pipe opening covered with coarse mesh, secured with well greased jubilee clip
flagstone
liner
earth
normal pond water level

soakaway pit or trench filled with rubble and covered by plastic sheeting, then top soil

caddisfly larva
|—————————————|
20mm

Plan four — a 2 basin pool

Willow, pruned to make it spread

Tall flowers

Bushes and saplings to rear

Tall flowers

Reeds or rushes

Water Crowfoot

Bushes

Tall flowers

Marsh Woundwort

Emergent plants

Emergent plants

Shorter flowers

Meadowsweet

Fringing plants

Water Mint or Purple Loosestrife

Fringing plants

Water Lilies

Butterbur

Slope of Land

Flagstones

N

Mini-ponds

It is worth mentioning here some other *ready-made* ponds, such as old baths, sinks, plastic or galvanised iron water tanks, old barrels, tubs, troughs and so on. All of these can be quite successful, especially if camouflaged inventively. Try a mix of 50% peat and 50% cement to disguise the outside of sinks etc. The great advantage is that the pond will be ready almost at once, and if you have the container, the cost will be minimal. Such a pond could well be an *extra* to your main pond, or a feature close to a window which will be appreciated by people unable to move around the garden easily.

Please bear in mind that even mini-ponds like these may be dangerous to animals or toddlers, especially slippery, steep-sided tanks. Incidentally, neither lead nor copper tanks are a good idea as these materials are toxic (though the layer of scale or oxide on their surface - acquired with age - makes them relatively safe). The same is true of brass, bronze and pewter which are also best avoided.

If you want **water** in your garden but are worried about safety, why not install a fountain in a tank, tub or half-barrel filled to the top with stones? The fountain will play attractively and the water run down through the stones to keep it supplied. Alternatively, a cascade could be constructed which ends in a similar stone filled pond. (Ask a qualified electrician to help with the wiring up of the pump - special care is of course needed for getting the supply to the outside location.) External pond pumps are sold by several suppliers and cost usually depends on how much water you want pumped per second.

Sometimes pond-making materials are available locally, free or at nominal cost. Examples might be dressed or rough stone, paving slabs, flagstones or old kerbstones (try your local council Highways Department for these), floortiles or slate, unwanted cast concrete shapes, or other such solid material. It makes sense to use these materials and incorporate them into pond construction. Stone and concrete is cheaper than concrete alone if your stone is free, and looks better! Make sure that the stone is non-porous though. Using the materials may take some thought - for example, worn flagstones make a lovely water cascade, hollow breeze blocks (no use for pond construction) will make good plant pots - the possibilities are endless.

5. Soakaway

Lastly, whatever method of construction you decide on, remember your pond is artificial: it will have to be maintained and topped up. If it rains heavily it may overflow, so a run-off channel should be provided, with a soakaway if possible. The diagram on page 8 gives a possible design. To avoid soil getting into the soakaway from above, put punctured plastic sheeting over the rubble before replacing the top soil layer.

Plan Five

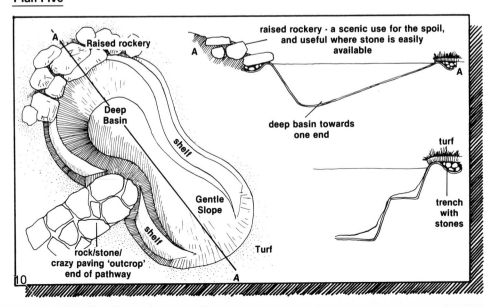

raised rockery - a scenic use for the spoil, and useful where stone is easily available

Raised rockery

Deep Basin

deep basin towards one end

shelf

Gentle Slope

shelf

turf

trench with stones

rock/stone/ crazy paving 'outcrop' end of pathway

Turf

3. Building your pond

The site
Often only one site is possible for a pond. In this case you must make the best of it, but if you do have a choice of sites, consider the following factors:

Safety
The safest site is one which is not hidden away or screened from sight. The very best site for a school pond is probably in good view of the staffroom window! This ought to cut down misuse of the pond, litter dumping and the incidence of children being pushed in. For a community site, position the pond in clear view of the road, though not too close to it. Hedges, trees and other *screens* invite problems. For a garden pond, place it to be seen easily from the kitchen or lounge windows.

wind direction

Spoil mound

Shelter
Placing a pond in the angle of some walls, or sheltered by a bank, helps to protect it from wind and extremes of frost. Check the prevailing wind direction, and position your spoil-heap bank in a curve to intercept it. Siting the pond under trees, however, is not a good idea since it may be too shady for vigorous plant growth and will tend to fill with leaves in the autumn. If not cleared, these can kill most of the life in the pond as they rot down, de-oxygenating the water.

Shade
A pond placed in a fully shaded position - such as north of a high wall - will seldom have a very attractive appearance. The water will be colder than a sunny pond and the productivity lower; at least it will evaporate more slowly than an exposed, sunny pond, which may lose a lot of water in a long, hot, dry spell of weather. Small ponds are most affected - larger ponds are probably deeper and so are less vulnerable. As a rule of thumb, try to position your pond so it gets at least half a day of full sun. Remember to check for tree and wall shadows at the pond site.

Slope
A pond in a natural hollow may tend to flood and overflow during wet weather. One sited in a natural run-off channel or stream bed may suffer scouring or be filled with debris during rain storms; either adversely affects the living organisms in the pond. For these reasons it is best to site the pond on a slight slope. This usually produces an attractive effect and makes it easy to arrange drainage, but may limit the shapes possible. A pond on a flat piece of ground can be any shape, but drainage is a little more difficult. A **marsh area** at one edge will provide an attractive extra soakaway.

Access
Remember that your pond must be accessible, both during the construction phase and later - for use (pond dipping or just enjoying) and maintenance. Think about this, in particular if you are using a mechanical digger, or having ready-mixed concrete or other heavy materials delivered. The ideal situation is accessible, but not too accessible - to avoid unwanted visitors such as vandals, large water-loving dogs and rubbish dumpers.

leech

60mm

Water

Check the nearest mains tap that can be connected up to a hose to fill and top-up your pond. Get its owner on your side, unless you have a stream available close by. Buckets or fire brigade are not the answer, though the Brigade may help fill the pond if you ask nicely!

Timing

The best time to build your pond is spring, so that it will have all the summer to get established. Ponds can be built at any time of year, as long as the weather permits, but building a pond in the winter is hard work.

Digging your pond

Having picked a site, decided on materials, checked for drains, cables, Roman remains and the like, and consulted with any appropriate interested parties, it is now time to organise your workforce and start a test pit - just a couple of spades wide and about as deep as you intend your pond to go. This should rapidly tell you what kind of soil you have, its depth and any likely problems.

The time taken to dig the test pit should allow you to make a rough estimate of the time necessary to dig the whole pond. (Allow a generous margin of error for fatigue and tea breaks.) Your test pit does not have to be within the area of the pond: filled with rubble it would make a good soakaway drain for an overflow.

Sectional plan for cast concrete pond

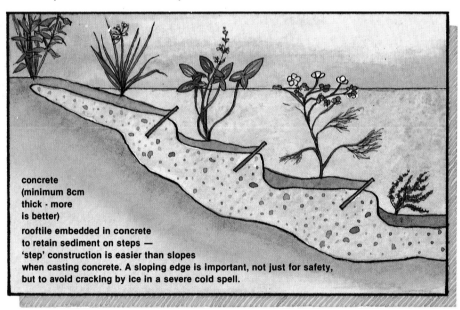

concrete
(minimum 8cm
thick - more
is better)

rooftile embedded in concrete
to retain sediment on steps —
'step' construction is easier than slopes
when casting concrete. A sloping edge is important, not just for safety,
but to avoid cracking by ice in a severe cold spell.

Assuming all has gone well up to now, the next stage is to mark out the area of your pond. Use one of the plans in the previous chapter - or your own variation. Remember the pond edges, perhaps a marsh area and plant borders, and paths all need thinking out, and drawing out on paper well in advance. Outline the pond shape with rope or tape and tiny wood pegs until you are satisfied that you have correctly marked it out. Take a long time over

freshwater shrimp
|—————————|
20mm

great waterboatman
|—————————|
16mm

this - slight adjustments and careful measurement now may save you a lot of digging later! Next paint round the cord with a white line - powder paint or whitewash - or run a line of sand along (less good as it spreads when trodden on). Remove the cord and pegs and make a final visual check of the shape.

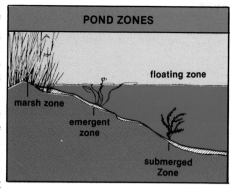

Now you are finally ready to start digging. Make sure that you have enough tools for everyone and that every digger knows the shape and depth profile of the pond. Remember that even quite large ponds don't need to be deeper than 80cm from the water surface. The important **plant shelf** should be about 25cm wide and 25cm below water level.

If the area is covered by turf, divide it up into squares by stretching strings across it, then use a sharp spade to cut the grass into equal sized turves. Use a shovel to lift the turves. Stack them carefully somewhere out of the way, as they will be useful later for covering the edges of the pond.

It is a good idea to have everybody involved in the project lift at least a few spadefuls of earth, as evidence of commitment; so they know how it feels, and so they can all say they helped to dig the pond. This is particularly true of children: however young, they should all be encouraged to make at least a token effort. It shouldn't be an adults-only enterprise. Make sure someone brings a camera or camcorder and everyone gets photographed doing their bit. Community groups might even want to contact the local paper and get the Mayor or Mayoress photographed lifting a shovelful.

Draining a concrete pond

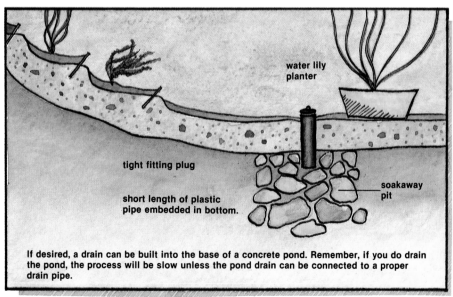

If desired, a drain can be built into the base of a concrete pond. Remember, if you do drain the pond, the process will be slow unless the pond drain can be connected to a proper drain pipe.

Stages in digging your pond

1. Mark out the shape and size on the grass with string, then chalk or paint.

2. Remove turves and stack fo use later as edging.

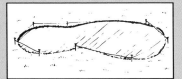

3. Check for level.

(a) Put tight strings across from pegs near the 'corners'. Tie or stick the strings so they do not slip up or down the pegs. For large ponds an extra central peg and additional strings are required. Tap in pegs until all strings are horizontal, tested using a builders' spirit level.

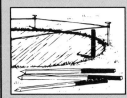

(b) Decide how far below string level you want the pond top (base of path or edging) to be. Mark sticks out with paint or waterproof felt pen, as shown. Knock in sticks near the corner pegs until their tops are just at string level, and add further sticks similarly marked anywhere on the outside strings, all at the same level. Keep these level markers just outside the area to be dug out. Finally remove the strings and corner pegs. Your marker sticks will tell you the level to dig to, even on a sloping site.

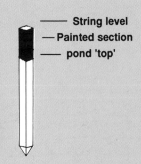

——— **String level**

— **Painted section**

——— **pond 'top'**

4. Decide on the main edge profile you want. Make a template from a piece of hardboard, cut full size to the pattern you want.

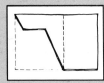

Use this as you dig to get the pond sides correctly sloped. (Examples of profiles are shown on the plans in chapter 2). Remember the margin shelf does not have to run all the way round the pond, but the sides should slope inwards at about 20° to avoid later subsidence. For safety, try to include one more gently sloping edge.

5. Dig out the hole, then smooth the sides and remove any sharp stones, etc. Cover the base and edges (after compacting with many pairs of feet) with about 3cm of sand. If using a liner, spread damp sand up the pond sides, or use layers of old newspaper, an old carpet, underfelt, plastic sheeting or even old fertiliser bags. This layer is to protect the liner from stones which may work out of the soil once water is put in the liner, and if your soil is stony, you may want to use a sand layer **and** old carpet, etc, for greater security.

Make sure the carpet layer extends over the edges of the pond and is continuous.

If you have the money, commercially produced protective sheeting is available for the same purpose.

In order not to let anyone over-exert themselves, change the digging, carrying and dumping teams regularly (or in the case of a family have lots of breaks for refreshment!). Try each job yourself to find out just how hard each task is. You will probably be surprised how heavy the work is, particularly if you have a clay soil to dig out. Try to get the digging phase over as quickly as possible - for one thing, it is less likely to rain if you take only a couple of days. It may seem ironic to have to empty a pond in order to get on constructing it, but it stops being funny and becomes tiresome very soon, and also decreases the enthusiasm of the builders. In fact, the longer the project takes, the less enthusiasm will remain. If the pond is a big one and bound to take a long time, try to do it in clear-cut stages, and hold team competitions for best progress in an hour or similar. Try to make the digging as much fun as possible. For a school pond, there will be opportunities for learning - soil profiles, roots, life in the soil, buried objects found - which all help to break up the routine.

Always dig a little deeper than you plan the pond to be - to allow for the lining and any sediment. Check the depth and slope profile regularly, as it is easier to get it right first time than to amend it later by putting *back* some soil. Compact the pond base carefully, especially for glass fibre or concrete lining.

Have your lining material ready to hand before the digging is finished. Not only is it frustrating to have to wait for it, but imagine how you would feel if the pond filled up overnight before the lining material arrived.

Lining your pond
This is the part of the project that takes most skill and care.

Glassfibre or rigid plastic ponds
If you are using one of these, make sure that it is the best possible fit by sculpting the hole and infilling where necessary. If it sags badly when filled, the edges will lift and the rigid liner will probably crack eventually. It is worth the time and trouble to get it right when first fitting.

Concrete lined ponds
If using concrete, try and obtain the services of someone skilled in casting concrete to supervise the job. The diagrams on *pages 12 and 13* show a suitable approach to constructing your pond with concrete, using *steps* made with old rooftiles.

An alternative method is to make the walls and base of the pond by laying down successive layers of heavy fabric (such as old carpet) and concrete. Several layers are required but build up rapidly to form a laminated wall. Finish with a final thicker layer of concrete to be sure it is waterproof. Soak the fabric first to ensure a good bond with the concrete, and take care not to crack it during the early stages. This method sounds odd but has the advantage that it is easy to form curves, bulges and slopes. If you are casting concrete, you may have to accept steps in place of slopes.

Remember, new concrete contains toxins which have to be thoroughly washed away, or sealed by painting over at least twice with *Silglaze* or similar. Either way, allow a few days for the concrete to set fully.

Next your concrete pond can be planted. It is a good idea to put a thin layer of soil in the bottom of the pond to provide nutrients and a substrate for bottom living organisms and rooted plants. Better still is to put in some mud and water from an existing, well established pond - this will contain eggs, seeds and the resting stages of many small organisms to get your pond off to a good start.

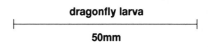

dragonfly larva

50mm

SECTIONAL VIEW OF A POND (CONSTRUCTED WITH A POND LINER)

Constructing the edge of a pond.

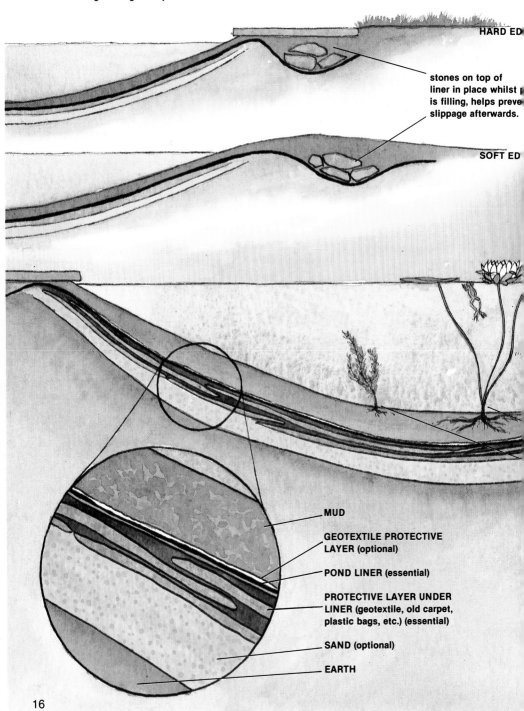

HARD ED

stones on top of
liner in place whilst
is filling, helps preve
slippage afterwards.

SOFT ED

MUD

GEOTEXTILE PROTECTIVE
LAYER (optional)

POND LINER (essential)

PROTECTIVE LAYER UNDER
LINER (geotextile, old carpet,
plastic bags, etc.) (essential)

SAND (optional)

EARTH

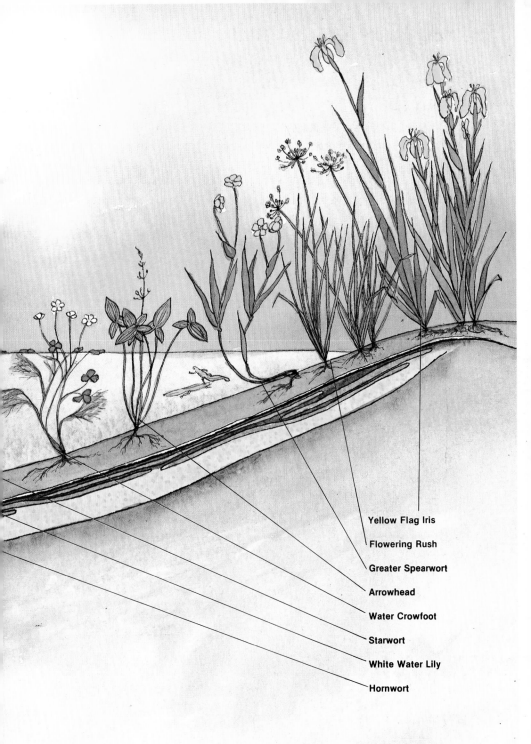

Yellow Flag Iris

Flowering Rush

Greater Spearwort

Arrowhead

Water Crowfoot

Starwort

White Water Lily

Hornwort

17

Flexible plastic or butyl rubber lined ponds

If you have chosen to use a liner in your pond, then this is the exciting part, after much sweat and backache. There are two slightly different approaches.

First the **fill and plant later** method ...

1. First, lift an extra line of turves from around the edge of your pond and prepare a trench about 15 to 20cm deep on this line.

2. Unroll the liner and spread it across the pond cavity; the more hands here the better. Try and get a reasonably even overlap around the pond edges and remember, you need more overlap where the pond is deepest. Let the liner sag into the pond cavity to check that it will fit correctly. Ideally you should have at least 50cm overlap all the way round.

    Assuming it fits, lay it flat across the pond cavity and stretch it on all sides a little, weighing it down on the edges with stones or bricks. These anchor the liner and will be 'dragged' towards the hole as the liner sags into it, so place them evenly and so they will not overhang the excavation.

3. Fetch the hose and turn it on (at last). As the liner fills it will gradually sag into the hole, stretching a little and also pulling the anchor stones inward. Most wrinkles will disappear, but those remaining will be covered by soil or plants later. Continue until the pond is full and the liner is moulded to the sides of the excavation.

4. Bed the liner in around the edge. This is why you lifted turves from around the edge and prepared your trench. Put the free edges of the liner into the trench and weigh them down with the stones or bricks, then level off with soil. If you have a lot of liner left, you can fold the edges loosely back into the pond (it helps to protect the liner) or cut off the surplus pieces if you prefer. Where there are awkward folds, nick the edges so that the material lies flat to the ground. Remember to leave a run-off channel so that excess water has a way out - to a soakaway or a boggy area.

5. Replace the turves, covering the edge of the pond and sloping down into the water to give a natural effect, or lay flagstones down around part of the edge to allow dry access. The flagstones should slightly overlap the pond edge (about 5cm), and slope very slightly down away from the pond edge. This is an important safety feature where children will make regular use of the pond. Flagstones should preferably be carefully bedded in sand and mortar, and joints should be filled with mortar to prevent plant growth — this is one place where safety comes before a natural finish!

6. Turn your beautifully clear pond into mud soup! Put in shovelfuls of sieved soil (no stones of course) so as to cover the base and the shelves of the pond fairly evenly to a depth of 5cm. Try to get some soil onto the sloping walls, and make sure you cover the edges above the water line to hide the liner from the sun. Leave to settle, then start planting, using baskets or directly into the soil layer. Left alone, the pond will clear in a few days at most and oxygenating (submerged) plants will complete the job.

Some pond builders advise a layer of protective sheeting on top of the liner. This does help but has one drawback, apart from the cost. If this sheeting is laid over the whole liner, including the edges of the pond, it tends to act like a wick, drawing water from the pond by capillary action and passing it to the surrounding soil. If it is only laid in the bottom of the pond this cannot happen, but it tends to slip down the sloping sides. For this reason I recommend simple sieved soil.

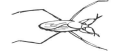

Pond Skater

|———————————|

16mm

Now for the other method - **plant before filling ...**

Dig the surround trench as before, but this time lower the liner into the hole and *leave* it there. Carefully push the liner into the corners (folding a little if necessary) and up the walls. At the surface place stone on the liner edges to hold them firm. Now, while the pond is still dry, put in the sieved soil on the base, up the walls and on the shelves. Spray water on the soil a little to help it stick. Now place your plant baskets as required, and put the rooted plants directly in the soil layer. If using several plant baskets, you may decide to add a soil layer only to parts of the shelves and pond base. You can add a submersible pump for fountain and/or cascade at this point if your design calls for it.

Once you are satisfied, then you are ready to fill the pond. It is easiest to use a hose for this, the end placed on a weighted plastic sheet in the lowest part of the pond so as to minimise disturbance of the soil layer. If you tie a string to the plastic sheet, you won't have to dive for it later.

Now is a good time to organise a sweepstake on how long it will take the pond to fill. If you don't have a hose you can try a bucket chain: if you have to fill it this way, try counting the buckets, it will help to pass the time.

Check the liner as the pond fills. It will settle into the shape of the hole, pulling the edges in a bit. Liners will stretch a little to fill the minor hollows or spread over bulges.

When the pond is getting full and the liner has settled to nearly its full extent you can start to bed it in around the edge trench, and lay turves and paving stones as detailed above,

Which approach should you choose? The second is probably best for butyl liners, but either will work. PVC liners, being more stretchy, may settle better using the first method. Either way, the pond will be murky for a while.

To give your pond a good start, try to put in a bucket of water and some mud from an existing healthy pond. This will add mini-beasts, eggs and seeds, but nature (courtesy of wind and birds) will do the same thing given time.

lesser waterboatman

|———————|
13mm

Marsh Woundwort

Flowering Rush

Marsh Marigold

Meadowsweet

Water Crowfoot

Greater Spearwort

Forget-me-not

A mound behind the po
topped by bushes and back
by trees, gives added shelt
Make sure tall plants do

Hard standing for visitors, pond dipping, etc

great diving beetle

32mm

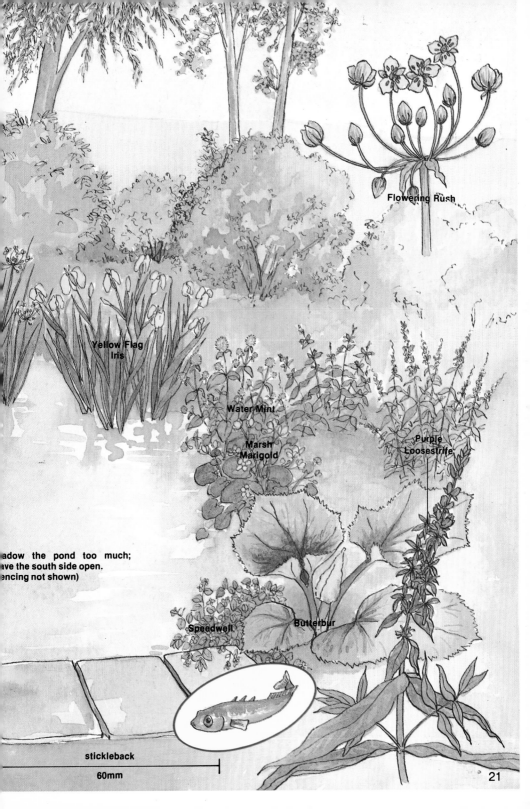

Flowering Rush

Yellow Flag Iris

Water Mint

Marsh Marigold

Purple Loosestrife

...adow the pond too much;
...ave the south side open.
...encing not shown)

Speedwell

Butterbur

stickleback

60mm

Settling

At first, new ponds look unattractive. The water will be muddy, may have scum on top and will very soon turn green. Don't worry, this happens to all ponds. The mud will settle, the water clear and pond animals will start to appear. Your pond will never be crystal clear, resembling a mountain tarn; if it is there is something wrong. A clear pond is a lifeless pond. It should not, however, smell. This happens to a pond with an excess of organic matter in it, which dies and decays, causing the smell. Your aim should be to strike a balance between plants, animals and open water for the best effect.

If you are not convinced of the need for some sediment and murkiness, some *untidy* fringing vegetation and soft, muddy pond edges, and instead picture a hard edged pond with clear water, a couple of artistically placed exotic water lilies and brightly coloured fish circling a central fountain, consider the following analogy. A *natural* pond is like a meadow, full of a variety of wild flowers and alive with bees, butterflies and insects. All it needs is to be mowed annually to maintain this life. An *ornamental* pond is like a lawn, limited to a few species of plants, most of which are considered to be weeds and discouraged, and very few animal species. In order to maintain its existence, it has to be fertilised, treated with weed killer, spiked, seeded and rolled and cut regularly

Although any pond is better than none, a *natural* wildlife pond holds far more than an ornamental one, and is easier to maintain. If you want goldfish and a fountain, why not build two ponds - one for each kind? (Notes on ornamental ponds are to be found in Chapter 6.)

Stocking a wildlife pond

Three types of large plants are found in ponds, corresponding to the pond zones shown on page 13: **emergent, floating leaved** and **submerged.** *Damp-loving* plants also grow around the edges of the pond (especially if you build in a marsh zone) and contribute to the visual effect, but these **fringing/marsh** plants are not truly pond plants.

Emergent plants
These have their roots in water but lift their leaves above it. Familiar examples will be *reeds* and *watercress.* In many books, these are called **marginals.**

Floating leaved plants
These are rooted plants, which have floating leaves and flowers, or they raise their flowers a little above the surface. *Water lilies* are the prime example.

Submerged plants
These grow wholly or substantially beneath the surface. A few bear flowers above the surface though they have submerged leaves and stems. The many *waterweeds* will be familiar examples.

Other plants found in ponds are the *algae,* which include microscopic, floating forms that frequently turn pond water green, or filamentous forms, the thin green threads which coat the sides of ponds and grow on plant stems. *Seaweeds* are algae too but no such large algae grow in fresh water.

Great Diving Beetle Larva

60mm

Also found in ponds are the non-rooted floating plants: *duckweeds, frogbit, water soldier* and *water hyacinth*. These can get to be a problem as they grow so fast.

The following list will help you in stocking your pond.

FRINGING/MARSH PLANTS

Recommended

Forget-me-not (Myosotis sps.)
Marsh Marigold or King Cup
  (Caltha palustris)
Meadowsweet (Filipendula ulmaria)
Skullcap (Scutellaria galericulata)
Purple Loosestrife (Lythrum salicaria)
Hemp Agrimony (Eupatorium cannabinum)
Greater Spearwort (Ranunculus lingua)
Marsh Woundwort (Stachys palustris)
Spear Mint (Mentha spicata)
Watermint (Mentha aquatica)
Peppermint (Mentha x piperita)
Brooklime (Veronica beccabunga)
Water Speedwell (Veronica anagallis-
  aquatica)

Not Recommended
Hemlock Water Dropwort (Oenanthe
  crocata)
  extremely posionous

EMERGENT PLANTS

Recommended

Flowering Rush (Butomus umbellatus)
Yellow Iris (Iris pseudacorus)
Arrowhead (Sagittaria sagittifolia)
Water Plantain (Alisma plantago-aquatica)
Watercress (Nasturtium officinale)
Water Violet (Hottonia palustris)
Bog Arum (Calla palustris)

* Can spread rapidly

+ Invasive, chokes ponds

FLOATING LEAVED PLANTS

Recommended

Fringed Water Lily (Nymphoides peltata)
White Water Lily (Nymphaea alba)
Amphibious Bistort * (Polygonum
  amphibium)
Frogbit (Hydrocharis morsus-ranae)
Water Crowfoot (Ranunculus aquatilis)

Not Recommended

Foreign waterlilies
Duckweed + (Lemna sps.)
Water-fern + (Azolla filiculoides)
Water Hyacinth +
  a tropical waterweed that chokes lakes
  and rivers; frost kills it

SUBMERGED PLANTS

Recommended
Hornwort (Ceratophyllum demersum)
Water Milfoil (Myriophyllum spicatum)
Bladderwort, a carnivorous plant (Utricularia
  vulgaris)
Water Starwort (Callitriche stagnalis)
Not Recommended
Canadian Pondweed (Elodea, Anacharis) +
New Zealand Pondweed (Pygmyweed) +

EMERGENT PLANTS

Not Recommended
Greater Reedmace +
  often wrongly called Bullrush
  (Typha latifolia)
Unbranched Burreed + (Sparganium
  simplex)
Marestail + (Hippuris vulgaris)
Common Reed + (Phragmites australis)

Planting - notes

Try to bed all fringing/marsh plants in well so that they do not become dislodged by the wind. Once they become established this will seldom be a problem: clumps of plants tend to support each other as their roots link to form a network. When planting, consider the eventual **height** that the various plants will grow to.

water louse

20mm

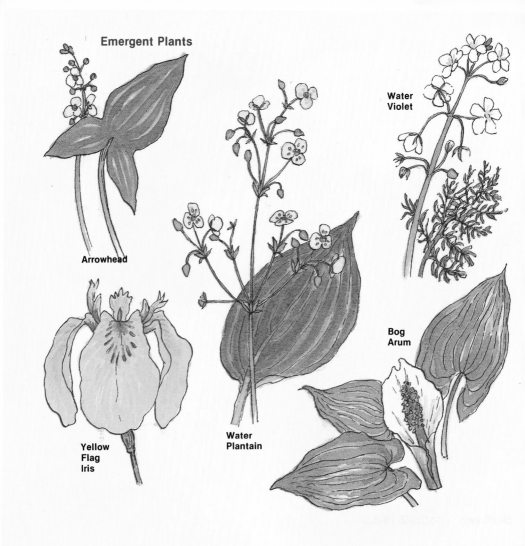

Emergent Plants

Water Violet

Arrowhead

Bog Arum

Yellow Flag Iris

Water Plantain

Emergent plants for the pond shelf

The common reed *(Phragmites australis)* can reach a height of nearly 3.5 metres (12 feet), though this is unlikely in a small pond. (This plant is known as the *Norfolk* reed which makes the best quality thatching material.) It will be better to plant lower growing reeds, rushes and sedges around the edge of your pond (in a marsh area or on the shelf). Attractive species are *flowering rush* which grows to about 1.5 metres and *yellow flag iris,* about 1.2 metres. If you feel no pond is complete without *reedmace* (often called *bullrush*) with its distinctive club-shaped flower heads, then try to plant the *lesser reedmace (Typha augustifolia)* rather than the *great reedmace (Typha latifolia)* as it is better scaled to a small pond and less rampant. Thin out regularly, or your pond will fill up with reeds!

Also on the pond shelf, try *arrowhead, water crowfoot, water violet* and *amphibious bistort.* Good marsh plants which like to *get their feet wet* are *marsh marigold* and

pond snail

40mm

ramshorn snail

30mm

24

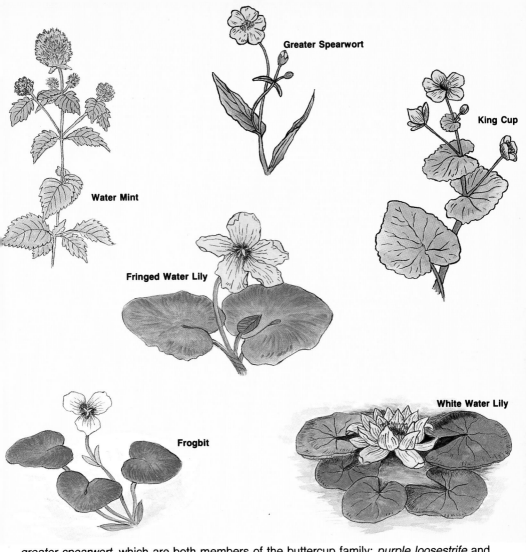

Greater Spearwort

King Cup

Water Mint

Fringed Water Lily

White Water Lily

Frogbit

greater spearwort, which are both members of the buttercup family; *purple loosestrife* and *marsh woundwort,* both with pinkish-purple flowers; *water mint, spear mint* and their hybrid *peppermint,* all with lilac-coloured flowers attractive to insects (and vigorous growth - keep an eye on them). *Watercress* can also be grown, but tends to get quickly out of hand. You can at least eat what you weed out!

Other attractive plants which will grow on the shelf at the edge of the pond are f*orget-me-not* (there are various species including a water forget-me-not) and several species of speedwell notably *brooklime* and *water speedwell.*

A sweet smelling plant of damp meadows is *meadowsweet,* which is recommended. Not quite so highly thought of is *Ransoms* or *wild garlic (Allium ursinium),* an attractive glossy green leaved plant with a head of white star shaped flowers but which smells strongly of garlic, especially if crushed.

damselfy larva

frog tadpole

30mm

40mm

25

Plants for the marsh area

On *page 23* you will see our list of suggested marsh plants, which can be positioned in a marshy border at the pond edge. I now give a few suggestions for interesting plants to include in this area.

Several **herbs** grow naturally on river banks and stream edges, and will thrive happily in your marsh area:

Soapwort (Saponaria officionalis) grows in full sun or light shade and reaches 45-100cm in height. Pale pink scented flowers appear in late summer. Sow the seeds in spring, or buy pot-grown from the garden centre. Once established, these will self-seed and return each year - cut back after flowering to get a second crop. Leaves, stems and roots can be boiled in rainwater which may then be used to wash hair, skin and delicate fabrics. Decorative flowers are useful in pot pouri. Note that *soapwort* should not be grown near fishponds, as the roots are highly poisonous to fish.

Chives (Allium shoenoprasum) grows in full sun or partial shade and likes moist, well-drained fertile soil. Keep watered in dry spells and fertilise annually. Green/yellow cylindrical leaves smell strongly of onions; the flowers are pink/purple and clover-like. Chop the leaves for salads, or infuse them in water and use as a spray against aphids, apple-scap and mildew.

Angelica (Angelica archangelica) grows naturally in damp meadows and likes deep moist soil and light shade. It reaches a height of 1 to 2.5 metres, so make sure you have room! Flowerheads can be dried for winter decoration; leaves can be stewed with acidic fruit to reduce the need for added sugar; stems can be crystallised for cake decoration. You will get a relaxing bath by adding a few leaves to bath water, or you might use them to brew herbal tea - which is a tonic against indigestion and travel sickness.

Marsh mallow (Althaea officionalis) likes full sun and moist fertile soil, and grows up to 2metres high. The flowers (July-September) are white/pink. Leaves and flowers should be dried quickly at high temperature and will then make an infusion which is useful in treatment of dry skin and sunburn.

Peppermint (Mentha piperita) likes warm, rich, moist alkaline soil and full sun. It grows to 60cm in height and has pale purple flowers from July to September. Thought to be a hybrid of watermint *(Mentha aquatica)* and spearmint *(Mentha spicata),* it can be grown easily from stem cuttings rooted in water. Use the leaves for herb tea and mint sauce. Grown near roses it will deter aphids and it is also useful to attract bees to colonise a new bee-hive.

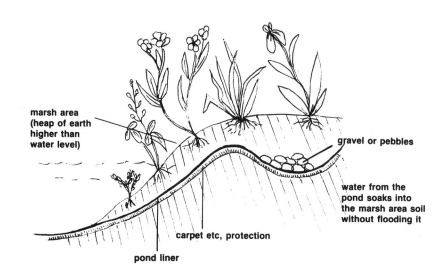

marsh area (heap of earth higher than water level)

gravel or pebbles

water from the pond soaks into the marsh area soil without flooding it

carpet etc, protection

pond liner

There are many **wildflowers** ideally suited to a marsh area. Here are three favourites:

Water forget-me-not (Myosotis scorpioides) is a low growing hardy perennial and likes damp soil and shade. It grows naturally throughout Britain and has flowers from May to September (usually blue but sometimes white or pink).

Yellow flag iris (Iris pseudacorus) is a tall plant with yellow flowers (June to August) which grows well in marshy ground or in fresh water (on your pond shelf). *Purple flag iris (Iris versicolor)* is medium height with purple flowers (June to July) and happy in the same conditions.

Marsh marigold (Caltha palustris) is also known as *King cup* - part of the buttercup family. It grows to 50cm tall in marshy ground and has yellow flowers (March to June).

If you have plenty of space and you would like a large interesting plant in your marsh area, try planting a specimen of *butterbur (Petasites hybridus)*. The growth form is a bit like rhubarb but the leaves can grow to nearly 1 metre wide. As this species has male and female flowers on separate plants, one specimen is unlikely to seed, but as a perennial, once established it will grow every year - and spread!

Several **garden flowers** also enjoy wet ground:

Astilbe (Astilbe arendsii) - really a range in the saxifrage family. Colours vary from white and cream to pink, purple and deep red. Heights are from 15cm to 1.5 metres; hardy perennials which flourish in damp soil with light shade.

Primula (Primula florindae) is a late flowering hardy variety with strong scent. Yellow flowers in July and August resemble giant cowslips. Likes moist soil or shallow water and reaches a height of 60 - 100cm.

Rodgersia (Pinnata superba) is another saxifrage family member and grows in sun or shade in damp peaty soil, reaching 1 to 1.5 metres high. It has large glossy leaves and fluffy flowerheads - pink, yellow or white. Prefers a sheltered position.

Mimulus (Mimulus luteus) grows in rich, moist soil to 30-50cm high. The flowers are scarlet, yellow or spotted (June - July).

Lobelia (Lobelia fulgens) has beautiful scarlet flower spikes and reddish-green leaves. It reaches 1 metre in height and likes wet conditions but is only half-hardy.

Whatever you plant, there will also be **natural colonisation.** This usually produces a pleasant effect, but *docks, thistles* and *nettles* may have to be removed by hand if they threaten to become dominant.

The above mentioned plants are given only as a guide to planting - many others are suitable, but in general, try to avoid exotic species. Native plants are more likely to attract and feed the mini-beasts, birds and insects which we are trying to attract. For this reason, native pond weeds (listed in our table as **submerged plants**) are preferable to (and more attractive than) Canadian pondweed or the invasive New Zealander *pygmyweed*, also called *Australian stonecrop (Crassula helmsii),* a real menace which has choked ponds in several parts of Britain.

stonefly larva

|——————————————|

25mm

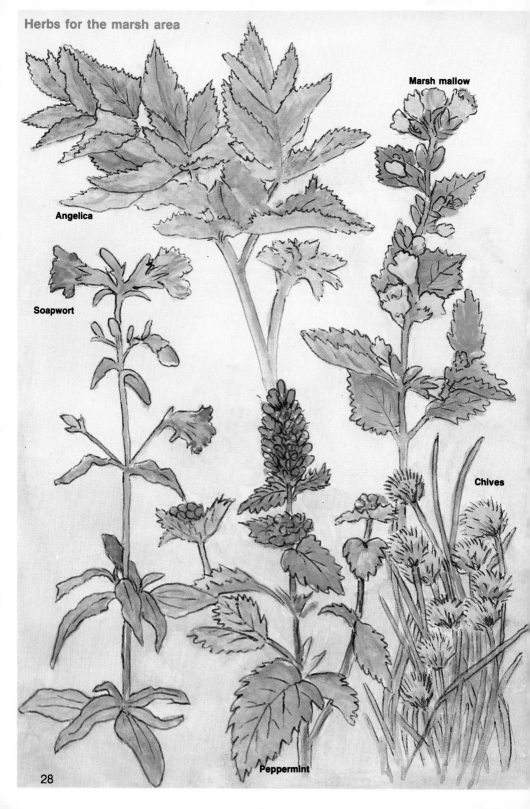

Angelica

Marsh mallow

Soapwort

Chives

Peppermint

28

Astilbe

Primula Florindae

Mimulus

Rodgersia

Lobelia fulgens

29

How to plant your pond

The best planting times are May to September - if possible May/June. Emergent plants can be planted directly into the soil layer on your pond shelf, or in shallow containers. Similarly, floating leaved and submerged plants can be put directly in the bottom soil or in larger containers. Remember that your plants will grow and spread - containers allow you a lot more control than direct planting.

The **aquatic plant containers** as shown here are widely available in a variety of shapes and sizes. They resemble plastic washing baskets, with many holes in the sides and base. First, line the container with a square of hessian, then fill nearly to the top with soil - heavy soil is best, or use ordinary garden soil. Don't use peat or leaf mould or sand. Plant one or more of your aquatics firmly into the soil, allowing for growth and keeping emergent, floating leaved and submerged plant types in separate containers. Add a good layer of gravel to the surface and carefully water the container before putting it in the pond.

For **water lilies,** keep the crown above soil level. For **emergents,** you should normally use a container slightly too large and put in just one plant - this will grow and can then be moved along your pond shelf to ensure good spacing round the pond.

Submerged plants are usually sold as pieces - make a hole in the soil and push the lower part of the stem in, then press the soil round it just firmly enough to hold it. A large container will hold (say) 15 submerged aquatics.

Planting containers in the pond should be done carefully and slowly so as not to disturb the top layer of gravel (which helps trap the soil in the container). Slowly lower emergent plants onto the shelf - usually a recommended depth below the surface will be shown on labels (when the plants have been purchased). If in doubt, keep to no more than 5cm below to begin with. You may need to put packing under the container - something which won't tear the liner. Wood blocks or bricks work well. Leave some space on the shelf for growth and try to put a label with each plant.

It is a good idea to **number** the containers (try waterproof label tapes or scratch deeply into a plastic label) and then to make a list of numbers and plants to keep separately. It is hard to remember the name of each plant - especially in the winter - and your record can include planting depth and date of planting. Labels in the pond are soon bleached by water and sun.

Containers for the **bottom** can go where you like, but *lilies* are best placed in a fairly shallow area (at least 45cm deep) or on bricks and gradually lowered as they grow so that their leaves always reach the surface. *Oxygenator* containers should be spread - in a small pond put a set quite near to each end of the pond. The aim should be to have around half of your water covered by foliage when the plants are fully grown. That leaves clear water to see into the pond through - and for the pond's health.

mosquito larva

10mm

For those who do not like wading, containers can be accurately placed using two stout ropes (eg. skipping ropes). Thread a rope through each side of the container so that two helpers can hold it up from opposite sides of the pond. Slowly transport it above the water to the desired spot, then sink it slowly by relaxing the ropes together (teamwork is essential!). When settled, drop one end of each rope and pull on the other end to release it. (For lilies, leave a plastic rope - perhaps a piece of clothes-line - attached to wooden pegs pushed in at each side. As long as these are undisturbed, you will be able to move the lilies to deeper water with ease, and finally remove the rope.)

Containers on the shelf are easily retrieved for plant care, and those in the depths can be hauled out (with great care) by using one or two garden rakes. Of course, this will disrupt the bottom quite a lot, so do it only in extremis. The containers will soon be hidden by plant growth, but they do place a limit on this growth. Pushing slow-release fertiliser tablets in the container soil may be useful as an annual spring feed, at least for plants that look in need of help.

How many plants?

As a rough guide, a new pond with a surface area of **3 square metres** might include:
2 lilies, 15 submerged/oxygenating plants and 6 emergents.

A pond of **10 square metres** could have:
3 floating leaved / lilies, 45 oxygenators and 15 emergents.

The submerged plants are most important as they provide ideal homes - and food - for many minibeasts, while keeping the water in good condition. Eventually, around *half* of the pond surface area should be covered by plants, but oxygenators tend to grow quickly, so do not overplant at first.

daphnia (waterflea)
⊢——⊣
3mm

water mite
⊢——⊣
4mm

Planting the surrounds of your pond.

It is a good idea to plan the planting round your pond. If you don't, something will grow anyway and it will probably be docks and nettles. By choosing your fringing vegetation carefully you can restrict access to the pond to one or two areas of bank and provide cover for plant life in others. Try to plant several species to get a varied effect but do not mix them together as some species will overwhelm others. Instead, start plants in groups or clumps of a single species. As they become established they will grow together for a more natural effect. Planting trees and bushes around a pond helps to shelter it from wind, give a natural backdrop and create a tranquil atmosphere but if they are too close they will create problems by dropping leaves in the pond and shading it from sunlight.

The **tree** species generally associated with ponds are the various types of willow, alder and aspen. *Willows* will grow extremely vigorously and respond to pruning by producing several stems when one is cut. In this way they will quickly hide a wall or provide shelter - at least while in leaf. Willow grows 2 to 3 metres in a year and regenerates so well that a cut branch pushed in the soil will often take root. *Alders* grow rapidly too and will quickly form a screen or windbreak. Although a rather gloomy dark green they are usually well shaped trees and bear interesting little cone-like seed cases and catkins. *Aspens* are more delicate trees, with light green leaves that move in the slightest breeze. They provide a pleasing contrast to alders. These three trees like damp ground, but other trees will grow close to ponds equally well.

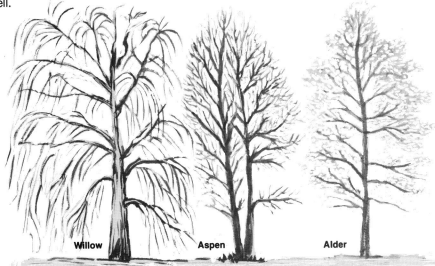

Willow   Aspen   Alder

Of course, almost all broad-leaved trees lose their leaves in winter, lessening their sheltering effect. Exceptions are *holly* and *holm oak* (evergreen oak) but both of these grow slowly. You could try *box* or *bay* - both evergreen - and fast growing *conifers* can be planted, though these have little to offer to wildlife except shelter. There are only three native British conifers: Scots pine, juniper and yew. *Scots pine* grows well in sandy or poor soil but has an open (rather than dense) branch structure. *Juniper* will grow in the harshest of conditions and produces edible berries. Its dense growth produces excellent cover too, but it is slow growing. *Yew* is a good shelter tree but it is **not** recommended because all parts of the tree are very poisonous, especially the attractive berries.

flatworm

18mm

33

Many sorts of **bushes** can be grown but avoid *laurels* and *rhododendrons* because they suppress the growth of other plants. *Privet* makes a surprisingly good shelter bush when allowed to grow; the flowers and fruit attract butterflies and birds as well. It has the advantage of being semi-evergreen though the berries are slightly poisonous to people. A very good shrub is *butcher's broom (Ruscus aculeatus)* - tough, spiny, evergreen, with orange-red berries: an attractive vandal repellent.

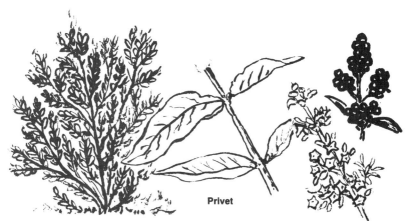

Privet

If your pond has a wall behind or beside it, why not train a **creeper** up it? A shady wall is good for *ivy,* which is evergreen and good for wildlife. A sunlit wall is suitable for a range of climbers both native and introduced. Fences can also provide a support for climbing plants. If you have a large ugly wall or fence to cover and require rapid screening, try *Russian vine.* The only problem with this plant is that it grows almost visibly fast and never seems to stop. Cut it back regularly!

Russian vine

Ivy

The choice of **ground cover** around the pond depends on the degree of *tidiness* required. Poor soil is an advantage if you want to encourage meadowland wild flowers. A good way to start a new meadow area is to use one of the grass/wildflower seed mixtures, which are designed to suit particular soil types. Always try to use seed of British origin. (See **Appendix** for suppliers.)

adult mayfly

|—————|
11mm

6. | Ornamental Ponds

Fishes are great attractions in ornamental ponds, but in wildlife ponds, they rapidly eat up the mini-beasts! The ideal way to have both is to construct separate ponds - of course one can be larger than the other. So, if you decide to have an ornamental pond as well as a wildlife pond, here is how to go about it.

Setting up your ornamental pond
The basic method of **construction** is the same, but as a natural appearance is not essential, choice of shape, profile and position are entirely up to you. A straight lined, geometric shape with a hard edge may give a better effect in a formal garden setting and a fountain can be put in; a feature that tends to jar in a naturalistic pond.

Formal rectangular pond

In any pond, however, safety should be a prime consideration. Sheer drops into deep water are dangerous, so a shelf below the edge is always a good idea. Vertical sides can easily be broken by ice expansion within a concrete pond, and a butyl, glass fibre or vinyl lined pond could be damaged in the same way.

You have a wider choice of **plants** for an ornamental pond - many exotic species are readily available from specialist suppliers and garden centres. For example, there are *water lilies* of many colours and sizes including miniatures that will grow in 12 inches of water. If you want to include fish, water lilies are a good idea as they will give shade on hot days. Similarly, a wide range of interesting exotic emergent plants are available, some with variegated foliage which gives a long lasting visual effect. To avoid plants spreading too far, it is best to restrict them to submerged plant baskets. Line the baskets with hessian and cover their surface with gravel, to avoid the soil or compost getting into the water. Wet the basket thoroughly before placing it in the pond, for the same reason.

adult damselfly

|-------------------------------|
35mm

35

Choosing the fish

Introduce **fish** to the pond only after the plants have been settled in, (a matter of 2-3 weeks) otherwise they will pull up your carefully placed plants. Suitable fish for ponds are *goldfish* of the hardier types, (the more exotic *lion-headed, bubble-eyed, globe-bodied* and *double-finned* varieties are at a disadvantage in a pond). *Shubumkins, golden* and *silver orfe* and - in a large pond - *koi carp* are fine also. Dark coloured fish are very difficult to see, so you will not get much enjoyment out of them. *Golden orfe* and *goldfish* live happily together and make a good contrast in form and motion. Some books recommend adding a scavenger, such as *catfish,* but this has its drawbacks. The *wels* or *European catfish* is the best suited to our climate, but it grows to huge size in favourable conditions and is omnivorous, large specimens eating sizeable fish and even ducks! It would not get so large in a garden pond but it might get large enough to eat your goldfish. A tench is a much more placid and suitable fish, and it is possible to buy golden tench, but as all tench are bottom dwellers you would not see it very often. Scavenging fishes should not really be necessary unless you over feed your fish. Goldfish and their carp family relatives tend to pick over the bottom anyway.

golden/silver orfe

shubumkin

koi carp

Feeding the fish

A few fish in a balanced pond with considerable vegetation do not really need feeding, but in the unnatural overcrowded conditions of a formal pond they will need supplementary food in spring and autumn. Do not feed at all in the winter. Excess food makes for cloudy water.

Cleaning the water

Keeping the water clear can be done in several ways. The most natural is to put in a few freshwater mussels, these will continuously filter the water, removing floating algae and bacteria as well as protozoa.

The only requirement for these mussels is some sediment or fine gravel for them to bury themselves in; a plant basket or pot would do. Otherwise you could use mechanical filtration, which requires a pump. If you want to put in a fountain or cascade, filtration can easily be combined with a submersible pump. A range of types are available from water garden supply companies.

Lastly, you can use algicides - chemical herbicides that selectively kill algae. If you use these, bear in mind that these are poisons, dangerous if misused. They probably will not do much for the health and vigour of your plants and fish either. For these reasons I do not recommend their use. Algal blooms are usually a sign that something is wrong with your pond, correcting the problem at source is better than treating the symptom, as the condition is likely to recur.

Overfeeding

A good growth of pond plants helps prevent algal problems, since the water plants remove nutrients from the water that the algae need. The usual cause of algal blooms in fish ponds is over feeding, which adds nutrients to the water, and can also cause other water fouling problems, notably cloudiness, unpleasant smells and de-oxygenation which will ultimately kill the fish. Most people overfeed fish, because the fish eat so voraciously that people assume they are hungry. Actually fish are opportunists, grabbing a meal whenever it is available. In the wild they would eat whatever is suitable, whenever it turned up irrespective of appetite. Fish do not need to be fed as regularly or as much as birds or mammals as they are cold-blooded, and do not have to use food energy to keep warm. Fish growth is related to food availability: they grow fast when food is plentiful but grow more slowly when food is scarce. The golden rule for feeding fish is, do not give more than they can eat in a few minutes, little and often is better than a lot at infrequent intervals.

A less formal pond arrangement

Fountains and Cascades

Moving water definitely adds an extra interest to a pond. A **fountain** looks good in a formal pond setting, but doesn't do waterlilies much good; they prefer still water, so it is best placed at the other end of the pond. It can also help oxygenate a pond and can be combined with a filter. The filters are easily set up using a submersible electric pump, and the pump merely has to be securely held in place at the right depth to be effective. A protected electricity supply is necessary, of course, and care should be taken to ensure that the pump inlet doesn't get blocked with debris, plants or unwary fish. Ensure that you protect people by having a safety cut-out (RCD) on the circuit connecting the pump.

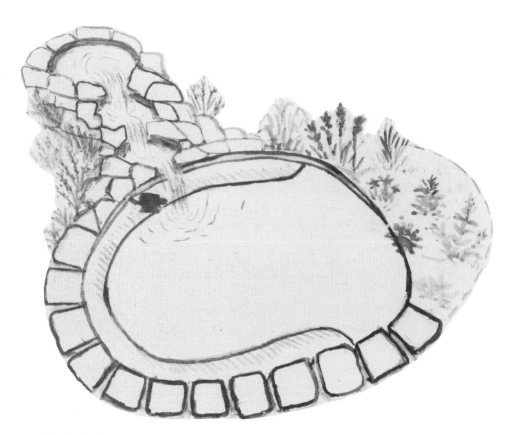

This design includes a cascade with water from a submerged pump.

adult dragonfly
105mm (across wings)

Another option is a **cascade.** This is a more natural looking feature and could be combined with a wildlife pond, but because of pump problems, is better combined with a semi-formal pond. A cascade requires a slope down to the pond, for which excavated soil could be the basis. A series of basins is then set into the slope, usually disguised with rocks and plants, and water is pumped from the pond via a hosepipe to the top basin and then spills from one basin to the next successively until it re-enters the pond. Hide the hosepipe by letting it emerge from the pond under the cascade. The pump is best placed on the pond shelf in easy reach, as you will want to take it out of the pond for maintenance in the winter months.

Position the pump on the pond shelf and run the water pipe up the edge of the cascade.

Cascades can be simple or elaborate, with mini-ponds as basins, sloping rock shelves, or there can be merely a single drop into the pond - a waterfall. The design is up to you, but a formal pond would look best with a severe, sculptural cascade of exposed basins, whereas a semi-formal one should look more like a natural stream cascading over rocks.

A raised pond

If you are starting from scratch and are worried about safety, you could consider a raised pond, built 60 to 90cm above ground level. This kind of pond is particularly suitable for use by people in wheelchairs as the water level is at a more convenient height. It is also appropriate in a warm, dry climate where wind carries dust across flat ground - the pond will be much less affected if raised above the ground. A raised pond is also good for a nursery school or a mother and toddler area and can be combined with a mesh cover.

A raised pond can allow access to all sides, and is one of the few opportunities in pond building to use brick. The broad top can provide seating or be a suitable place to put information about the pond or what can be found in it. You won't need to excavate the pond - except for the wall foundations - but you will need to line the inside well if you use a pond liner. An alternative is to use concrete (constructed by shuttered walls) and then build an external brick wall.

A raised pond can also be built out from a slope, so that it can have a natural appearance at the sloping end (a good site for a cascade) and a more formal look at the other.

adult caddisfly

├─────────────┤
20mm

Safety

Safety has already been mentioned several times, but a few other things should be said on this topic. All ponds are potentially dangerous, as an unconscious person can drown in a couple of inches of water and breathing in one lung-full of water will quickly induce unconsciousness. Also, people drown more quickly in freshwater than sea water; as sea water in the lungs takes water out of the blood concentrating it, which is a slow process, whereas freshwater in the lungs passes into the blood, diluting it and causing the heart to fail because of increased blood pressure, which is a more rapid process.

Having said this, drownings in garden ponds are very rare, (swimming pools are much more dangerous), and good design can minimise the danger. What if you inherit a pond with dangerous features - steep sides, slippery slopes, hard edges, a drop to the water level, sloping surrounds, etc? The best thing to do would be to change things if possible by making edges shallow and gently sloping, removing hard edges, reducing depth by infilling, preventing access at certain points and other remedial actions, but if this is not possible, what then?

Small ponds can be covered by wire mesh on frames or by welded steel grids (a good use for a discarded gate or set of railings), which can be locked in position onto steel posts driven into the ground or set into concrete. Such grids should be made to be openable when desired for pond dipping or maintenance. This may seem drastic but might be essential in some places.

I would recommend this for a pond in an area used by handicapped children for example, who might have difficulty getting out of shallow water or even of attracting attention if they fell in.

adult mosquito

|———|
9mm

41

7.	**Animals and your pond**

Very soon after your pond has been filled you will begin to see life in it. New ponds go through a series of changes with early colonisers giving way to later arrivals. This is an example of ecological succession.

Normally, the first organisms to appear will be microscopic *algae,* whose spores arrive carried by the wind. Exactly which kind will appear in the water is largely governed by chance. Some kinds, particularly the colonial forms, are large enough to be seen with a hand lens; others require a low powered microscope. After this, the first animal forms will usually arrive though flying insects like *water boatmen* or *beetles* can appear even before the pond is full of water.

Sometimes the algae seems to take over and *blanket weed* swamps the new pond and turns it bright green. Raking will help but be patient and the problem should correct itself. If you introduce water, mud and plants from other ponds, small animals will come as well - including the *snails* which will help control algae. If necessary, put in a few *pond mussels* - they feed on algae by filtering them out of the water.

It will take time, though, for a varied population of living organisms to colonise your pond. Many of the pioneer species are microscopic and new ponds characteristically hold large numbers of a relatively few species. Older ponds have more diverse populations but often fewer numbers of any one species. It is best to allow your pond to settle and stock itself with animal life during the first year. You will see changes in its water, plant and animal populations and it will come to a fairly stable ecological balance. Winter is a resting period for pond life, but spring will reveal a rich population, almost certainly with unexpected species present.

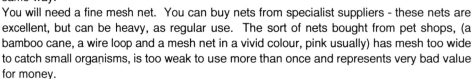

Dipping

You can keep an eye on the way that a new pond develops by regularly sampling it and noting the changes. Comparing with another pond can be interesting too, because no two ponds develop in exactly the same way.

You will need a fine mesh net. You can buy nets from specialist suppliers - these nets are excellent, but can be heavy, as regular use. The sort of nets bought from pet shops, (a bamboo cane, a wire loop and a mesh net in a vivid colour, pink usually) has mesh too wide to catch small organisms, is too weak to use more than once and represents very bad value for money.

To make your own net you need a broomstick, a wire loop (coathanger), and a cloth net (nylon net curtain remnant). Bend the wire and attach with jubilee clips. Next, strongly sew your net in an open, quite deep bag shape, and then fold back and sew over the wire loop.

whirligig beetle larva

14mm

Other equipment

Once you have used your net to collect samples from your pond, you will need something to sort your catch out in, and a shallow white tray is ideal. The kind of plastic tray that microwave ready meals come in is excellent. To actually hold your catch for examination, use several clear, wide mouthed plastic jars with lids.

For sorting out your catch in the tray, plastic spoons and eye droppers are ideal, but require a bit of practice. Tweezers are difficult to use without killing the creature you are trying to lift. Lenses or magnifying glasses are very useful, as many pond animals are very small, or need to be looked at closely to be identified.

How to use a net

Using a net properly takes a little practice. Don't splash as you put the net in - be gentle or the creatures will swim rapidly away! Move it smoothly through the water, turn the net around, and sweep it smoothly back, continuing by lifting the net out of the water.

Take your full net to the sorting tray (not the tray to the net!) and turn it over and inside out, into the tray, already partly filled with clean pond water. Wash the net out by dipping it into the water in the tray. Be sure that you have emptied the

Emptying into a tray

corners of the net. It is always best to let small animals fall or swim out of the net. Try not to pick them up in your fingers as they are very fragile and easily killed.

Identifying your catch

Wash out large plant material in the tray to shake off clinging pond animals, then remove it back to the pond. Let any mud settle and then look carefully at your catch. Some animals are very difficult to see until they move. Use a plastic spoon or an eye dropper to move animals or pieces of plants from the tray to water-filled jars. Fish can jump, some insects can fly, and snails and leeches can climb the sides of jars, so put the tops on.

Pond plants and animals can be kept for a while in a large jar or an aquarium, but are better returned to the pond, where they can grow, feed and breed. To return your catch, gently submerge the sorting tray in the water and let the animals swim out. Try to return all pond organisms to the same area that you got them from, as many creatures are vulnerable away from cover.

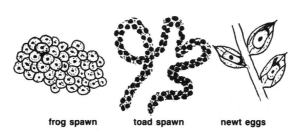

frog spawn   toad spawn   newt eggs

Animals in your new pond

What can you expect to find in a new pond? Microscopic floating green specks, ranging up to forms the size of a pin head. Some swim! You need a good high powered lens or a low powered microscope to see detail of even the largest forms, but if you can get to see them, many have fascinating, intricate shapes. One of the largest is *volvox,* a colonial alga, which is a lattice work ball of regularly spaced individual members, each with 2 beating 'tails' or flagellae which moves the whole colony through the water like a rolling ball. There are many others - enough for a specialist book or three!

Of course, several quite visible mini-beasts will appear within days/weeks of filling. The drawings throughout this book give at least the main types of mini-beasts you may find in your pond. As the years go by, the dominant types will change but there should be a good range of species after the first year.

Pollution indicators

Some plants and animals are important in that they can tell you how clean or how polluted a water body is. A *stonefly larva* indicates a very clean pond indeed! Good collections of *water beetles, water boatmen, damselfly larvae, freshwater shrimp* and *caddisfly larvae* indicate a satisfactory and normal pond with a low level of pollution.

However, lots of *water fleas, water lice, bloodworms, mosquito larvae* and *sludgeworms* are a danger signal that your water may be getting very polluted. Plants can also be indicators; a wide variety of vigorous plants shows clean water, limited numbers of a few types, yellowing leaves and very little underwater growth is a bad sign.

Great-Crested Newt

Common Newt

Palmate Newt

Reptiles

Adders prefer dry conditions and are unlikely to visit your pond. The harmless *grass snake* is more fond of water - it is a member of the water snake family and eats many frogs. However, if you see a snake near the pond, it is most likely to be the legless lizard *slowworm* seeking slugs and snails.

Amphibians

Native British amphibians will probably find and colonise your pond naturally. If not (because your pond is too far away for them to find) then a jam jar of frog or toad spawn will soon fill your pond with tadpoles. Toad spawn is laid in long strings rather than the large blobs of frog spawn. A gently sloping exit from the pond (as in a marshy area) will allow baby frogs and toads to leave the pond when they are ready.

There are three types of *newt* in Britain - the *common* or *smooth,* the *great-crested,* and the *palmate. Newts* lay their eggs singly on the leaves of water weeds and are becoming rarer, so do look after any you find in your pond. You may be able to find eggs or animals in a friend's pond to stock your own - this will be a real contribution to the continuance of the species in Britain. It is illegal to take great-crested newts (or natterjack toads) from the wild as both are now endangered species.

Of course, frog and newt tadpoles will not survive the attentions of fish so a wildlife pond should not include fish, except perhaps *sticklebacks.* Amphibians like shade, so lilies, oxygenators and emergents should cover (when the pond is mature) around half the water surface.

Adding *terrapins* or other non-native species is not recommended - climate is not right and neither is the supply of food animals/plants. You will get your best out of a wildlife pond by sticking with nature's choice of native animals and plants. When you turn to your ornamental pond, then anything goes - but you will have to assist the survival of exotic species.

Toad   Frog

Birds

Fish ponds may receive visits from fish eating birds. You probably won't see the Loch Garten *Ospreys* (which use a local trout farm as their favourite take-away) but a *heron* is quite likely to drop in at even a small suburban garden pond. It seems a shame to discourage such an impressive bird from calling in, but one heron can clear your pond of fish quite quickly. They usually make their visits at dawn or whenever the area is quiet, so the first evidence may be missing fish and telltale foot prints in the mud. Herons can be deterred by stringing nylon line or black cotton or pegs around the edge of the pond at about 15cm height. Herons always land on solid ground and then wade into the water or stand at the edge, so the threads will put them off.

Ducks are more difficult to deter, as are *seagulls*. If a pair of ducks take up residence, they will quickly clear your pond of almost everything edible, and they will eat a very great range of foods! They will also trample the edge and foul the water. The same thing will happen even faster if *Canada Geese* decide to take up residence. These opportunistic and aggressive birds are increasing in numbers, particularly in the South of England and regard all water bodies as their personal, private property. They take a lot of convincing that you have a prior claim to your pond and I would advise you not to let them get settled!

Many *garden birds* will be attracted to your pond - they will do little harm but will certainly like shallows (perhaps the edge of the marsh area) where they can bathe. Adding your pond to the garden will mean that you will see and enjoy many more birds. They benefit from native plants around the pond and perching positions and undergrowth nearby. They will also be glad if you keep the pet cat away!

Swallows and *house martins* may visit to gather mud for nest-building, and *sparrows, blackbirds, wagtails, starlings* and *pigeons* will probably want to drink and bathe. You will also see several other species, according to the area of the country and how near you are to woodland.

Mammals

Fish eating *mammals* are not likely visitors (except for that domestic cat). A chicken wire, weldmesh or chain fencing link cover is the only sure protection against cats. A visit from an *otter* is a very unlikely possibility, as it is virtually extinct in many parts of the U.K., though it seems to be gradually increasing its range and numbers at the moment. However, more likely in some areas is a visit from a feral *mink*. Mink are water loving animals, almost as at home in the water as otters and just as fond of fish. A mink could be a troublesome visitor, and as with cats, only a secure well fitted cover would be a deterrent. The only other fish eating mammals that could visit are the native *polecat,* in the central Wales area or nearby English Counties or feral *ferrets,* now living in several different areas of the country. Neither of these is a specialist fish catcher but will take the opportunity to grab a fish if it appears.

The vegetarian *water vole* may make your pond home but should not be a problem. *Foxes* do not catch fish but would certainly eat fish if they could get them. Like *squirrels, mice, bats* and *rabbits,* they may be attracted for a brief drink. A bigger problem may be the pet dog - I know of at least one dog who fancies a long drink and a swim every time she sees our pond!

Maintenance and problems

A pond does not require much maintenance but it does need to be regularly checked for leaks, contamination and litter. If litter is removed promptly, the pond will look better and people will tend to respect it more. Otherwise litter will breed more litter and the pond may become completely choked with the stuff. Of course, this will also block up any pump you have fitted, causing a burn-out or failure.

Contaminated water

It is best to keep the **water level** in a pond relatively constant - this allows plants and animals to grow best and limits the chances of weeds and grasses getting a hold in the strip between the water surface and the pond edge. Topping up can be done with tap water or any other convenient source of clean water. If chlorine from tap water builds up (perhaps after a dry spell) and starts to affect the pond life, try running a water pump (with fountain or cascade) or bubble air through with an air pump to oxygenate the water.

If some other form of contamination is suspected, the only real remedy is to drain the pond and refill it, after checking the bottom for any residue of contamination. In really severe cases, you may have to clean out all the bottom sediment and replace with fresh soil, though I have never heard of an example this bad. Try to save all the plants and animals you can - even small cuttings, after thorough washing, will help get the pond started again.

Leaks in your pond

In the case of a **leak,** let the water subside until the hole becomes visible. Small holes may have to be searched for. Normally such holes can be sealed in situ, with a patch of liner material and a suitable adhesive - available from the liner supplier.

If the hole is at the bottom you may have to bail out the last of the water to find it. In any case, try to refill the pond promptly as many mini-beats will survive a short period of drying. If the bottom is disturbed badly, you may get an *algal bloom* when the pond is refilled - this is because nutrients have been released from the bottom sediments. Like other algal blooms this is a self-correcting condition, though removing filamentous algae (blanket weed) will help. A wooden pronged rake is safer than a metal one, of course. Compost the removed algae (or any other plant matter you take out of the pond).

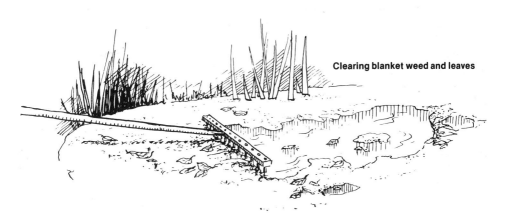

Clearing blanket weed and leaves

Plant roots and your liner

Some pond plants such as reeds may be so vigorous that they push **roots** through the liner. In this case there may not be much of a leak as the root is likely to expand with the sudden new source of food! However, if you pull the plant out or it dies ... Using plant baskets can reduce this problem considerably, especially if you move them regularly and keep the plants to a reasonable size.

More dangerous to the liner is the growth of plants outside the pond which force themselves **in** through the liner! This can happen where coarse grasses such as *couch-grass* push root-runners under and then through the pond liner. They seem to like the resulting muddy patch and grow up to the light to become a new plant species in your pond. Of course, *couch-grass* does not give up easily, and you will have quite a battle and many holes to patch. The best solution is to remove all signs of such weeds before the liner goes in - both under the liner and all round its edges. Keep a sharp watch for new growth round the edges and remove it before it becomes troublesome.

Autumn leaves

The most important maintenance job is clearing the fallen leaves from the pond each autumn. If there has been a good growth of fringing and submerged vegetation during the summer, then thin and clear this - it will grow back next spring. The above-water parts of reeds and rushes should be substantially cut back too. They die anyway in the winter and re-grow from the root stocks. Don't neglect this annual job (even if it is not needed in the first year or two of the pond's life) or the water may become stagnant, pond animals could die and the open water may be choked.

Just as a meadow needs mowing or a garden needs weeding, so a pond requires an annual clearance to maintain its condition. It is the fate of all lowland ponds eventually to fill with vegetation, become marshes, then carse (alder) woods and eventually, mixed broadleaf woodland. This is the natural process of *succession*. However, one regular clearance a year is sufficient to maintain a healthy, balanced pond, full of aquatic life. Enjoy it!

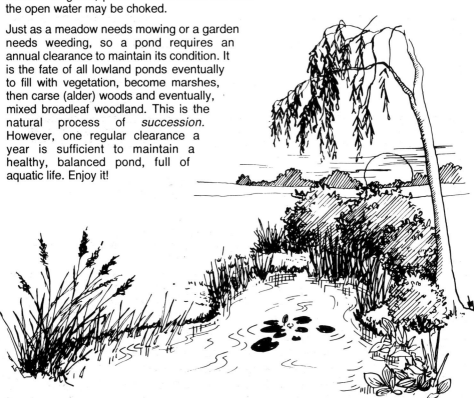